Color in Fashion

Color in Fashion

Color in Fashion
Copyright © 2009 by **maomao** publications

Asian edition published in 2009 by:
Page One Publishing Pte Ltd
20 Kaki Bukit View
Kaki Bukit Techpark II
Singapore 415956
Tel.: [65] 6742-2088
Fax: [65] 6744-2088
enquiries@pageonegroup.com
www.pageonegroup.com

First published in 2009 by **maomao** publications

Text copyright © 2009 by **maomao** publications
Design & layout © 2009 by **maomao** publications

Publisher: Paco Asensio
Editorial Coordination: Anja Llorella Oriol
Editor: Macarena San Martín, Estel Vilaseca
Texts: Macarena San Martín, Charo Mora
English translation: Heather Bagott
Copyediting: Peter Ridding
Art Direction: Emma Termes Parera
Layout: Enrique Casp Bellver, Raquel Marín Álvarez

Editorial Project:
maomao publications
Tallers, 22 bis, 3º 1ª
08001 Barcelona, Spain
Tel.: +34 93 481 57 22
Fax: +34 93 317 42 08
mao@maomaopublications.com

ISBN: 978-981-245-714-1

Printed and bound in Spain

Contents

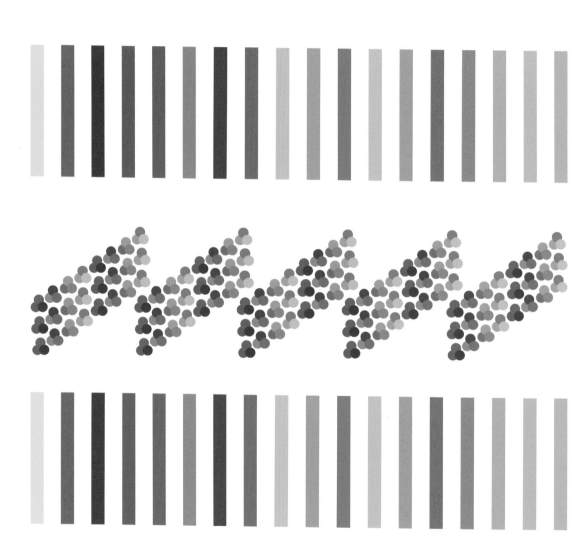

Color in Fashion

by Charo Mora

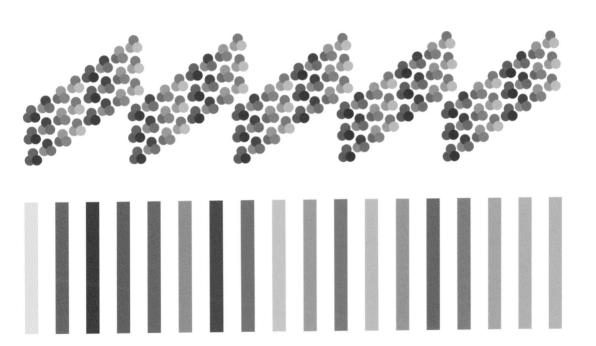

It would be impossible to imagine 20th century fashion without the yellow of Poiret, the blue of Lanvin, the black of Balenciaga or the black and white of Chanel; without the red of Valentino, the shocking pink of Schiaparelli, the futuristic white of Courrèges or the conceptual white of Margiela. The fashion scene just wouldn't be the same without the blending of colors by designers such as Emanuel Ungaro and Japanese designer, KENZO – greatly inspired by flowers – the daring combinations of orange, fuchsia and red of Yves Saint Laurent and Christian Lacroix – inspired by Matisse – or the green of Josep Font.

Fashion in the 20th and 21st centuries is typified by these designers and the unique and fascinating relationship that their retinas have with certain chromatic images. Interesting combinations which have created new formulas applicable to fashion result from the relationship these creators have established with color. This is a unique, personal adventure on which each stylist embarks with his color palette, which is then syntonized to develop shape, volume and ultimately his universe. In the hands of designers and artists, color is the cloak under which reality is transformed into a more harmonious place. As well as being a source of inspiration, this factor becomes their personal stamp such as the green in Hooper, earthy colors in Rembrandt and the blue of Yves Klein.

And in the beginning there was color

Color explains and covers everything as it is omnipresent. At the beginning of the century of enlightenment, Isaac Newton discovered that solar light is composed of seven different frequencies: red, orange, yellow, green, blue, indigo and violet. It was an important discovery in physics which corresponded to the colors of the rainbow – a natural phenomenon, difficult to explain for the first men on earth, and which continues to captivate our retinas.

The first human experiences of color perception date back to the beginning of time. It was an era where one could imagine primitive man's fascination for the array of colors in a bird's plumage and an animal's skin and his desire to posses them, to have their beauty, strength and color. Natural attributes and animal characteristics were there to be imitated and embellished by man. This intelligent almost voyeuristic animal was inventive enough to challenge their beauty. His imperfections spurred his creativity and perhaps the least blessed of all the creatures built beautiful peacock tail-like decorative features with his own hands.

Color as a privilege

In the early days of history color was rare. Dyes and pigments were scarce and hard to obtain which explains why only the privileged few enjoyed them. For example, to obtain just one gram of purple pigment, more than 10,000 murex shellfish had to be ground and crushed – the best specimens were from the city of Tyre in Lebanon. Consequently this became the color of eastern luxury and a show of wealth that was recorded in ancient chronicles as being reserved for Persian kings, Jewish priests, and Roman emperors and subsequently for the highest ecclesiastical ranks. The common people and slaves were strictly forbidden in most cultures to use color freely – it was only for the privileged few. In Rome it was easy to distinguish the plebeians by the neutral colors of their tunics which barely covered their knees. They were made in colorless cotton, hemp, linen and wool.

However, the patricians ambled around their stylish villas wrapped in luxurious garments of orange, blue or bright green, giving them a more distinguished and elegant air. Color in the Roman Empire also provided an important code system for the toga – one of the garments which best symbolized their values. For funeral ceremonies the black-colored toga (*atra*) was used, the white toga (*virile*) was used to welcome the new patricians, the purple toga (*picta*) was only to be used by

© Bill Georgoussis

the emperor, and finally the translucent white toga (*candida*) was for those aspiring to enter the Roman Senate. With the fall of the empire, Christianity, which denounced luxury and carnal demonstrations identifiable with decadent Rome, opted for a much more basic, less sophisticated look and encouraged the custom of wearing natural non-dyed garments as a symbol of the new spirituality. The dress of Christians was like that of the Roman slaves – simple, austere and without color.

With the disappearance of purple at the end of the Byzantine Empire, red became the color of royalty. After the American conquest, this bright color was extracted from cochineal (also known as scarlet), providing a greater amount of longer lasting pigment. Thus the color red became cheaper and so ceased to be exclusive to the European courts. In the 15th century the Duke of Burgundy, Philip III the Good, introduced black into fashion – a color which had historically been the symbol of the Omeya dynasty. Edward of Woodstock was known as the Black Prince, due to the color of his fearsome and unmistakable armor. Philip the Good always favored this intense color since it enhanced the jewels in his armor, an effect which the Spanish court of the 16th century would promote years later, thus converting the use of solemn black into a symbol of its power and empire during the reign of the Austrian-Hapsburg dynasty.

Since the 17th century, the color black has been a constant feature in western wardrobes on both sides of the Atlantic – especially among the large emerging social group of the bourgeoisie. Verguin in 1863 discovered the aniline black dye which greatly increased the use of this elegant color among the masses. This paved the way for its arrival in the 20th century where it became the color of choice among contemporary men and women.

Colors in freedom

The revolution, which had taken place in the mind and retina of contemporary man regarding the foreword-thinking artistic movement in the first decade of the 20th century, soon reached the designers' studios — especially those who dared to experiment with colors that tradition and the canons of good taste had led to being banished from the wardrobe. As the avant-garde art movement recaptured the use of unmixed primary colors and restored a style of painting which was not subject to the mimetic representation of reality, it is no wonder that this innovative philosophy towards reality and color would influence the world of fashion.

This led to the development of Fauvism benefiting artists such as Raoul Dufy and Matisse. Naturally this resulted in these color visionaries collaborating with Paul Poiret, the revolutionary creator, who in the beginning of the 20th century not only liberated women from their corsets but also pioneered the use of vibrant and luminous colors, inspired by the Russian ballets designed by Léon Bakst. With this innovative vision, the 20th century ushered in a color palette inspired by flowers reminiscent of the *Belle Époque*, using pastel and mauve colors. Poiret went on to use red, yellow and green with oriental inspiration and an avant-garde vision, aiming to seduce rather than provoke or disturb the ultra-conservative retina of the bourgeoisie. The verbal and chromatic attacks of the Futurism movement were directed at this very class: Giacomo Balla in *Il vestito antineutrale* (*The Antineutral Dress*, 1914) proclaimed that the style of the modern man should above all be anti-bourgeoisie and thus asymmetrical with the use of bold colors such as yellow. Although the proposal never came to fruition, except within Futurist circles, it has been reworked by contemporary designers such as Vivienne Westwood, Bernhard Willhelm and Henrik Vibskov.

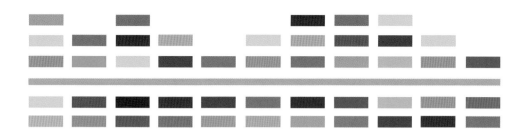

Art has brought greater freedom to the fashion world, encouraging it to question tradition and not take itself too seriously, thus enabling experimentation with elements of which it is composed: materials, shape and undoubtedly color. Elsa Schiaparelli – who never studied fashion although she graduated in philosophy – is perhaps the designer who has most successfully developed this aspect, being a clear inspiration for the fashion lines of Gaultier, Moschino, Galliano, McQueen and Viktor & Rolf. The Italian creator was daring with nearly everything: she made plastic jewelry, dyed natural skins, made patterns from newspaper motifs, radiographs and tattoos. She also patented the shocking pink color with which she decorated her boutique in La Place Vendôme, for which Salvador Dalí designed the chair inspired by the lips of Mae West.

In the decade of the twenties it was a Ukrainian artist, Sonia Delaunay, who would take the definitive step by deciding to unleash her creativity upon fashion. Delaunay applied theories from Orphic Cubism to her fabrics, exquisite pieces on which – for the first time since the days of cavemen – red, yellow and blue could exist together in an almost mystic pattern of circles, rhombuses and spirals. The work of Delaunay did not fall on hallowed ground, and color enthusiasts, such as American Ossie Clark and contemporary stylists such as Miuccia Prada and Consuelo Castiglione – designer for the Italian firm Marni – have been inspired by her talent in designing patterns and collections. Art may also have influenced the close relationships that designers have forged with certain colors, a typical feature of the 20th century. For example, the blue of Lanvin – a color which represents "home", and with which the French designer decorated her studio in the thirties – originates from a Fra Angelico painting which she saw on a trip to Florence and which her retina could never again ignore. The admiration that Basque couturier, Balenciaga, held for the Tenebrist colors of Zurbarán, Velázquez and the most tragic Goya influenced his work immensely. The designer ingeniously juggled the use of austere and elegant black as well as lacework and jet-black designs, giving

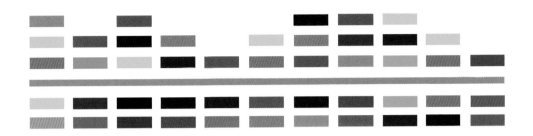

these traditional Spanish elements a universal appeal. His love of black led him to design an entire collection in this color which he presented in 1949 to a recently liberated and downtrodden Paris.

But he was neither the first nor the last to do so. Gabrielle Chanel in the twenties was already promoting the use of black for daytime while she encouraged pastel colors for evening wear. She was, with her talent and attitude, the architect of a new feminine style where comfort was not sacrificed in the name of aesthetics and thus women at the beginning of the 20th century were finally able to dress themselves unaided. In the twenties she created a black dress which the American press heralded as a "Ford T" (an allusion to the car), which became an essential part of any girl's wardrobe and still is – "the little black dress". Existentialists and the counterculture movement, appearing in the sixties, dressed themselves from head to toe in black as a sign of nonconformity, in reaction to a society that neither understood nor accepted them. This provoked a feeling which would never again disappear from those living in a capitalist society, be it punks or New York brokers, highlighting black as the color of modernity. Japanese Yohji Yamamoto and Rei Kawakubo, with their particular sense of aesthetics and fashion, would re-create this feeling by introducing a very austere and imaginative style characterized by the recurrence of the color black. Yamamoto states in an interview for *The Sunday Times* in February 1989: "I only wear black and navy blue", and Kawakubo declares he works with "three shades of black" – a real manifesto.

Today color in fashion is paramount, with trends pointing towards total yellow, a look with the same intensity as the contrast of black and white which Chanel formulated in her time and navy blue which Armani has made universal. Young designers – to whose work the following pages are dedicated – are a good example of the freedom of codes and combinations which with color is worked by the new generations. The 21st century is dressed in color. Let's enjoy it.

38

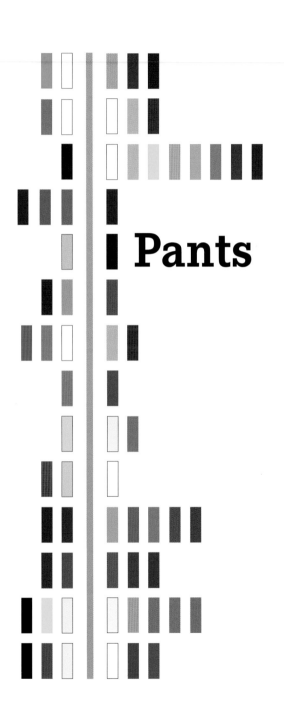

Pants

Classic pants

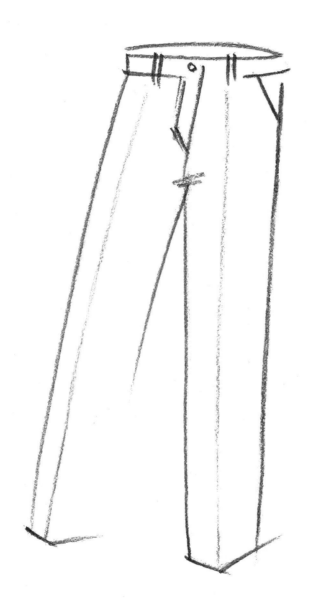

Bimbeau Delux *Le mans* www.bimbeaudelux.com

Photo © Hugo de la Rosa; styling: Cris M.Faber; styling assistant: Jorge Bolado Moo; hair and make-up: Silvia Luque; clothes: Martin Lamothe

Martin Lamothe *Sandokan*, SS 2008 www.martinlamothe.es

© Steffen Schulte

be0I SS 2008 www.be0I.com

Fitted pants

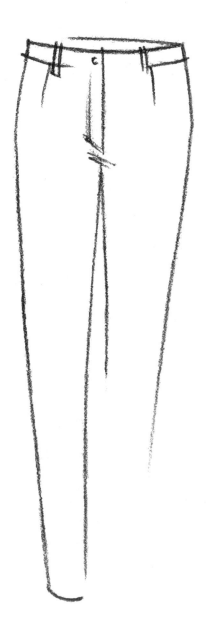

EBP *Tomorrow*, SS 2008 www.eduardballester.com

© Javi Morán

Alexis Mabille SS 2008 www.alexismabille.com

Photo © Hugo de la Rosa; styling: Cris M.Faber; styling assistant: Jorge Bolado Moo; hair and make-up: Silvia Luque; clothes: Martin Lamothe

Martin Lamothe *Sandokan*, SS 2008 www.martinlamothe.es

Susanne Guldager AW 2007-2008 www.susanneguldager.dk

Susanne Guldager

Which colors stand out the most in your collections?
Each color in its own perfect context.

What are your sources of inspiration?
I have a feeling or a thought that keeps coming back to my mind,
whenever I'm designing a new collection. It can be a social or political
thought, a historical period or simply just a shape that fascinates me. I
believe you can find inspiration in anything as long as you're willing to
be immersed in the subject.

Which is your favorite color?
Black. Black is simple.

Hareem pants

Txell Miras AW 2007-2008 www.txellmiras.eu

Photo © Nacho Alegre; styling: Cris M.Faber; hair and make-up: Silvia Luque; clothes: Martin Lamothe

Martin Lamothe *Rubriks*, AW 2007-2008
www.martinlamothe.es

Martin Lamothe

Which colors stand out the most in your collections?
All of them – it depends on the collection. My collections are
developed around colors; first I see splashes of color and then I
combine them until I have the shape, so it really depends on my
inspiration. What really stand out are the unique color combinations I
create – which is one of my goals. The more colors, the merrier!

What are your sources of inspiration?
Music, photography and places I've visited. Things which create a
focus on color – by way of its character or interpretation in the case of
music – or simply in a visual manner as with photography and
landscape.

What is your favorite color?
The color mustard because it is simultaneously warm and masculine,
earthy and ordinary as well as being difficult and conceptual.
Consequently it's the intelligent alternative to brown and it combines
with the palette of colors that appeals to me: pinks, mints, grays…
that is why it's the only color which I haven't yet used, but soon, very
soon, I will.

Pleated pants

Yiyí Gutz SS 2008 www.yiyigutz.es, www.myspace.com/yiyigutz

© Paolo Bocchese

Luxoir *Mirage*, SS 2008 www.luxoir.com

Pasarela Cibeles

Jose Castro AW 2007-2008 www.castroestudio.com

Photo © Cecilia Duarte; styling: Yolanda Armengol; make-up: Maria Caray; model: Alex

Walter Van Beirendonck SS 2008 www.waltervanbeirendonck.com

© Ronald Stoops

Walter Van Beirendonck

Which colors stand out the most in your collections?
I love all fresh colors. I like to combine and put them together just by "feeling" their intensity/cooperation together.

What are your sources of inspiration?
Ever since I read the book *Snow Crash* in the mid nineties, avatars have been fascinating to me. In my view, the ability to project oneself as a digital fantasy is the final evolution in the process of body manipulation. Leaving the physical body behind and acting, living, becoming a pure digital life form could be a logical evolution in future life forms.
With the arrival of Second Life, avatars have finally found their own world, and now the real world has become aware of the power of avatars. *Sexclown*, my SS 2008 collection, combines this new digital life form with another all-time, classic fascination of mine, fetishism, a theme that makes a strong comeback in my work.

Which is your favorite color?
For the moment, it's green, because it is fresh and reflects nature! Orange, red, yellow, light blue... love them all!

Cropped pants

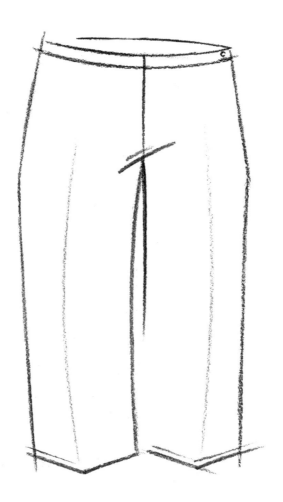

38

Alexis Mabille AW 2007-2008 www.alexismabille.com

Fabrics Interseason SS 2007 www.fabrics.at

© Maria Ziegelböck

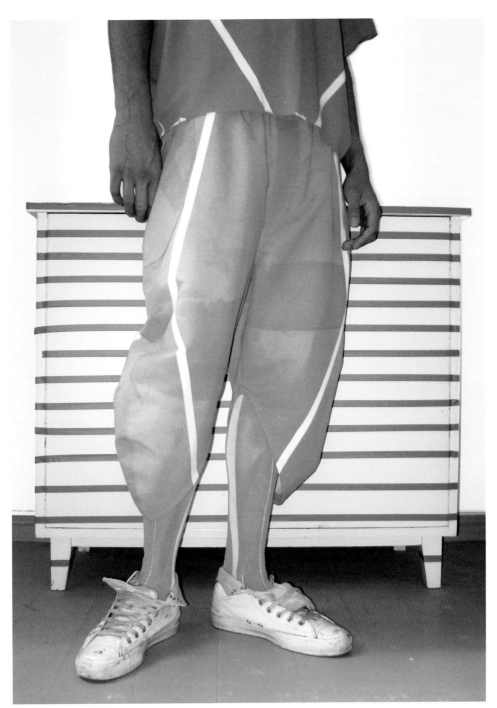

ANNTIAN SS 2007 www.anntian.de

Je Suis Belle SS 2008 jesuisbelle.hu

Susanne Guldager SS 2007 www.susanneguldager.dk

© Fredrik Säll

Shorts

BadaBing! SS 2008 www.badabingfashion.eu

Luxoir *Mirage*, SS 2008 www.luxoir.com

Easton Pearson SS 2007 www.eastonpearson.com

jesuisbelle

Je Suis Belle SS 2006 jesuisbelle.hu

Graphic design: Tibi Kiss

Olivia Rubin SS 2008
www.oliviarubinlondon.com

Sunshine & Shadow SS 2008
www.sunshineandshadow.com

© EXU

Playsuit

EMDAL colorknit, Susanne Guldager *Fresh Soft Square*, SS 2007
www.emdalcolorknit.dk, www.susanneguldager.dk

Susanne Guldager AW 2007-2008 www.susanneguldager.dk

Photo © Viel Sol; styling: Carlos Trujillo; glasses: Rebornshades, Martin Lamothe; clothes: Martin Lamothe

Martin Lamothe *Sandokan II*, AW 2008-2009 www.martinlamothe.es

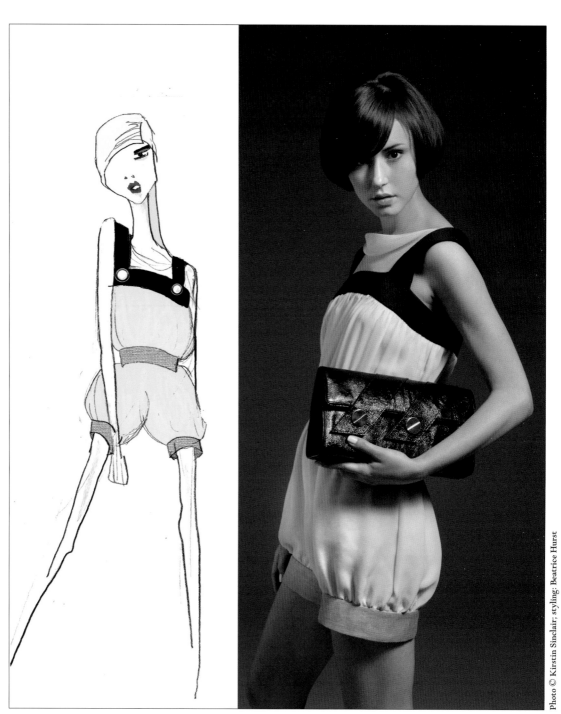

Olivia Rubin SS 2008 www.oliviarubinlondon.com

Ashish SS 2007 www.ashish.co.uk

57

Skirts

Pencil skirt

Karen Walker SS 2007 www.karenwalker.com

Beige SS 2008 www.beige.ch

© Daniel Sutter

Kirstimairie AW 2008-2009 www.kirstimairie.com

Photo © Sean Mcmenomy; styling: Drew Cornthwaite

ANNTIAN AW 2008-2009 www.anntian.de

ANNTIAN

Which colors stand out the most in your collections?
There's no outstanding one in particular! It always depends on the
topics we're working on.

What are your sources of inspiration?
Science fiction, every day life, art, music, pop, real life, nature,
techniques and progress... In general, ANNTIAN is inspired by
cutting-edge developments, by areas where things are in motion or
where they start to wake.
ANNTIAN is also highly inspired by people and their characters,
which give clothes a totally unique expression. So what really counts
is the person that wears a piece of cloth, and gives its appearance a
meaning!

Which is your favorite color?
We love all the colors and the variety you can get by mixing them. No
color will ever be the same! Oh, yellow is still something confusing for
us...

Classic pleated skirt

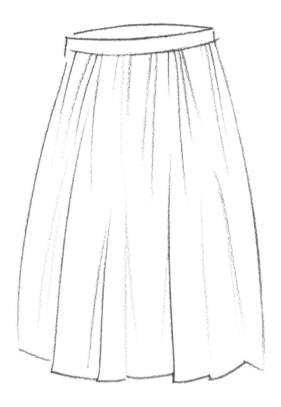

Tata-Naka AW 2007-2008 www.tatanaka.com

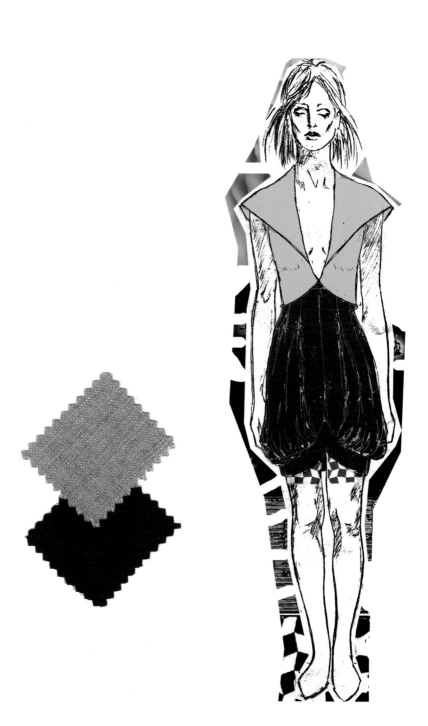

Romina Karamanea SS 2007 www.rominakaramanea.com

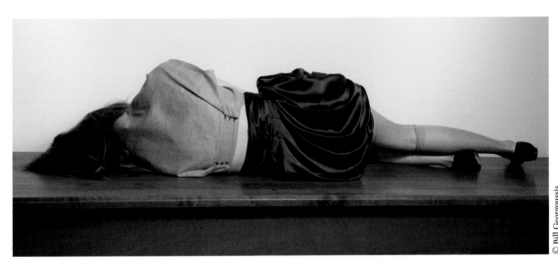

Romina Karamanea SS 2007 www.rominakaramanea.com

Skirt with front pleat

Easton Pearson SS 2007 www.eastonpearson.com

71

Mark Liu AW 2008-2009 www.stique.com

Photo © Snježana Josipović; hair and make-up: Nina The Headresser;
model: Flo

BiteMyStyle by Zoran Aragović SS 2007 www.bitemystyle.com.hr

Edwina Hörl AW 2006-2007 www.edwinahoerl.com

Photo © Seiji Shibuya; art direction: so+ba; styling: Kumiko Iijima/Cube;

Edwina Hörl

Which colors stand out the most in your collections?
In this particular collection, it's indigo, the color of the traditional
indigo dyed blue print fabric from Hungary. In general the collection is
a very colorful mix of traditional fabrics and colors from Central and
Eastern Europe.

What are your sources of inspiration?
This is an "evergreen" collection, celebrating the start of my brand
Edwina Hörl 10 years ago. It celebrates the rediscovery of my
Austrian culture and multicultural traditions. It embodies a humorous
mix of elements from Central and Eastern Europe: artistic handicraft,
like handmade straw shoes from Austria and embroidered fabrics from
Czech and Switzerland. I picked up clothing themes and silhouettes
that are frequently inspired by what ordinary people wear in these
regions, like aprons or the Sunday suit. The collection is a review and
a preview, containing stories oscillating between *The Sound of Music*
and "the smile of Japan".

Which is your favorite color?
Blue, recently yellow.

Tulip skirt

Hartmann Nordenholz AW 2007-2008 www.hartmannnordenholz.com

H Fredriksson AW 2007-2008 www.hfredriksson.com

© H Fredriksson

H Fredriksson AW 2007-2008 www.hfredriksson.com

Karen Walker SS 2007 www.karenwalker.com

Karen Walker

Which colors stand out the most in your collections?
We work with opposites in every area of our work and the colors we
seem to come back to again and again are bright ones like scarlet and
orange, thrown together with more murky colors like khaki and
taupe.

What are your sources of inspiration?
Again it's all about the opposites for us, and we look for colors that
contrast in their mood and approach.

Which is your favorite color?
Scarlet, cobalt and dusty pink because they're like coloring-book
colors; they're strong and there's no complexity to them – they're
totally up front.

Bubble skirt

PPQ AW 2008-2009 www.ppqclothing.com

BiteMyStyle by Zoran Aragović AW 2007 www.bitemystyle.com.hr

Photo © Tanja Bjelić; hair and make-up: Nina The Headresser; model: Flo

Je Suis Belle AW 2007 jesuisbelle.hu

Graphic design: Tibi Kiss

Txell Miras AW 2008-2009 www.txellmiras.eu

Txell Miras

Which colors stand out the most in your collections?
Black, white, natural colors and muted tones in general. When I am in creative mode I focus on shape as I tend to work without color to avoid distractions.

What are your sources of inspiration?
My inspiration comes from the things which interest me such as cinema, books, music and art. This is where I draw the conceptual inspiration from, whereas the shape is always developed in the studio through personal experimentation.

What is your favorite color?
Black. I have always found it to be a neutral and elegant color.

Tiered skirt

PPQ AW 2008-2009 www.ppqclothing.com

© PPQ

Bryce d'Anicé Aime AW 2008-2009 www.bryce-danice-aime.com

zazo&brull AW 2005-2006 www.zazobrull.com

Bora Aksu AW 2007-2008 www.boraaksu.com

Bora Aksu

Which colors stand out the most in your collections?
Purples, fuchsias, reds. I love the effect of splashing outstanding colors
into a muted color palette.
My AW 2007-2008 collection was a collection of warm eggplants and
fuchsias with contrasting silver grey.

What are your sources of inspiration?
I always start out with something very personal like childhood
reminiscences. Then other elements follow. For example, I mix a pinch
of punk, a pinch of Edwardian and a pinch of dream to make a dress.
For my AW 2007-2008 collection, nomadic warriors inspired the
shapes. The feminine shapes with harder materials such as leather and
metal were the essence of the collection.

Which is your favorite color?
I have two favorites: gray and purple. I love the fact that they are
really complementary with the skin tones and also create contrasts
with other color shades. I also really like the colors that belie
description. When you see a color but cannot label it instantly such as
"this is red or green", this also draws me to it… The colors in
between other colors also quite attractive.

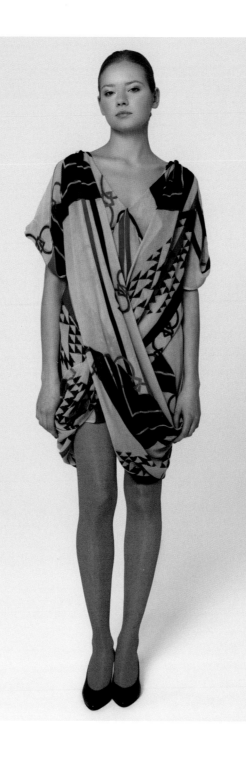

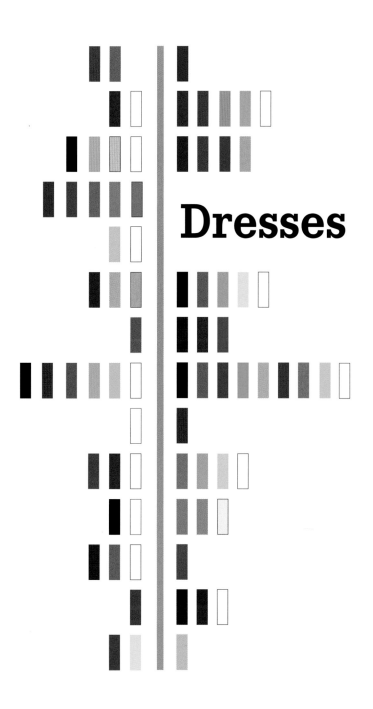

Dresses

Princess dress

Louis de Gama AW 2005-2006 www.louisdegama.com

PPQ AW 2008-2009 www.ppqclothing.com

Photo © James Mountford; styling: Darren Knight; hair: Gow Tanaka; make-up: Kim Brown; model: Gabriella/Select

Steve J & Yoni P SS 2008 www.stevejandyonip.com

Photo © Othello De Souza Hartley; styling: Davina Hawthorne; make-up: Mildred Padilla; dress by Davina Hawthorne; 2 Sword headpiece: DH Millinery; creature on headpiece: Pinaki Studios

Davina Hawthorne & DH Millinery SS 2008 www.davinahawthorne.com

Davina Hawthorne

Which colors stand out the most in your collections?
The color of the sunset from my studio window – maybe because I see
it on a daily basis. It is the most beautiful color and so hard to
describe as it is constantly changing. You really have to experience it.
Warm, surreal, beautiful and ever changing along the city skyline, it's
truly wonderful!

What are your sources of inspiration?
I like to see the contrast and differences between everything. This is
my inspiration, hard/soft, masculine/feminine. Also narrative and
debate in culture and society are important factors.
For my SS 2008 collection in particular, the inspiration was a mix of
armor, the floral and handcrafts. Recycled flower were hand painted
with gold and then beaded and embroidered. The collection displays a
multitude of color changing subtly from layers upon layers of dirty
blue, red and orange florals to intense bright gold.

Which is your favorite color?
I don't have one. It depends on the day, event, time, location or how I
am feeling at the time. I love the way color sounds, smells, tastes,
looks make you feel! The way it is perceived when you look at it and
touch it. Color is material and texture. It is life!

Beach dress

Easton Pearson *Cruise,* 2007 www.eastonpearson.com

La marthe SS 2007 www.lamarthe.es

La marthe

Which colors stand out the most in your collections?
Warm grays, grayish browns, stone colors and dirty pastel colors,
because to me they are modern yet romantic classics. They are also
somewhat avant-garde, natural and classy. I like the fact they're
"difficult" colors and thus quite rare. Being lackluster they require
contrasts which can create unexpected effects.

What are your sources of inspiration?
For my SS 2007 collection I drew inspiration from some modernist
style mosaics by a Catalan artist. The textures, the colors and the
pictorial theme itself encouraged me to pleat the fabric and cut the
garments in very specific ways. Actually I was also influenced by a
very extreme silhouette that I saw in a film from the eighties. Sharon
Stone was wearing a long suit jacket and a mini skirt which was
completely hidden at the back by the jacket. It was incredibly sexy! I
wanted to create a smoother version of it – the same look but
something fresher and more romantic.

Which is your favorite color?
Stone gray because it accurately represents the concepts described in
the first question. It works wonders when you allow yourself to be
seduced by its coldness.

Tunic dress

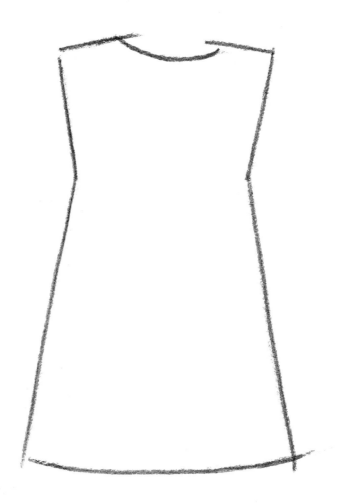

Hartmann Nordenholz AW 2007-2008 www.hartmannnordenholz.com

Ziad Ghanem SS 2007 www.ziadghanem.co.uk

© Ram Shergill

Easton Pearson SS 2007 www.eastonpearson.com

Mini dress ruched at waist

Mark Liu AW 2008-2009 www.stique.com

Bernhard Willhelm Women's collection, SS 2008 www.totemfashion.com

Ana Šekularac AW 2008-2009 www.anasekularac.com

Yiyí Gutz SS 2008 www.yiyigutz.es, www.myspace.com/yiyigutz

Yiyí Gutz SS 2008 www.yiyigutz.es, www.myspace.com/yiyigutz

Little black dress

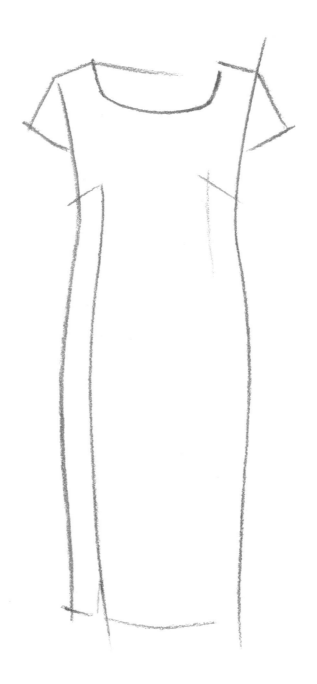

Romina Karamanea SS 2007 www.rominakaramanea.com

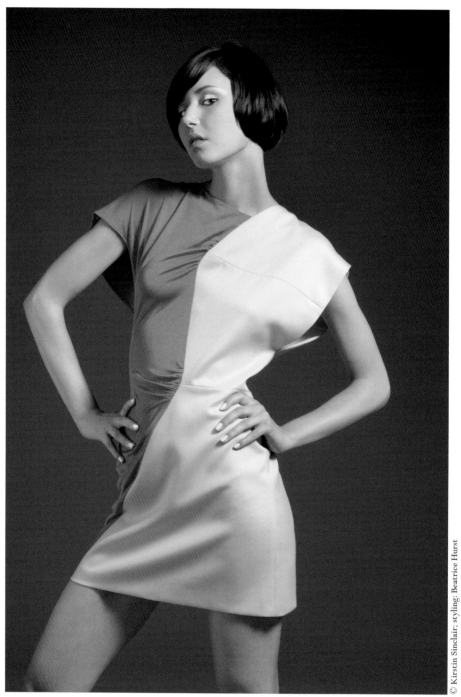

Olivia Rubin SS 2008 www.oliviarubinlondon.com

Hampus Bernhoff SS 2008-2009 www.hampusbernhoff.com

Bernhard Willhelm Women's collection, SS 2008 www.totemfashion.com

© Maria Ziegelböck

c.neeon AW 2007-2008 cneeon.de

Boho dress

Leonard AW 2006-2007 www.leonard-paris.com

Bernhard Willhelm Women's collection, SS 2008 www.totemfashion.com

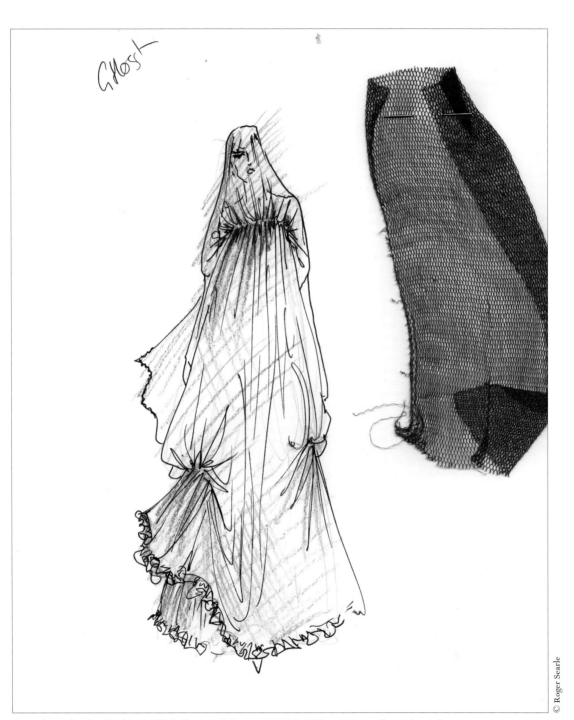

Roger Searle for Camilla Staerk *The Influence of Ghosts*, AW 2007-2008 www.camillastaerk.co.uk

Allegra Hicks SS 2007 www.allegrahicks.com

Allegra Hicks

Which colors stand out the most in your collections?
The strength of my prints comes from the use of color. I team
saturated colors with muted, organic ones to generate the mood of
each collection.

What are your sources of inspiration?
Close observations of nature; leaves, insects and shells inspire my
work. By manipulating the image, using a range of media, the result is
an abstract illustration from which I derive my prints.

Which is your favorite color?
I enjoy working with purples and aquas, golds and silvers. Their
versatility allows me to combine these intense colors with chic, earthy
tones to bring a sophisticated, modern feeling to my collection of
prints.

Uniform dress

Swash SS 2007 www.swash.co.uk

© Koomi Kim

Claudia Rosa Lukas AW 2005-2006 www.lukas-by.com

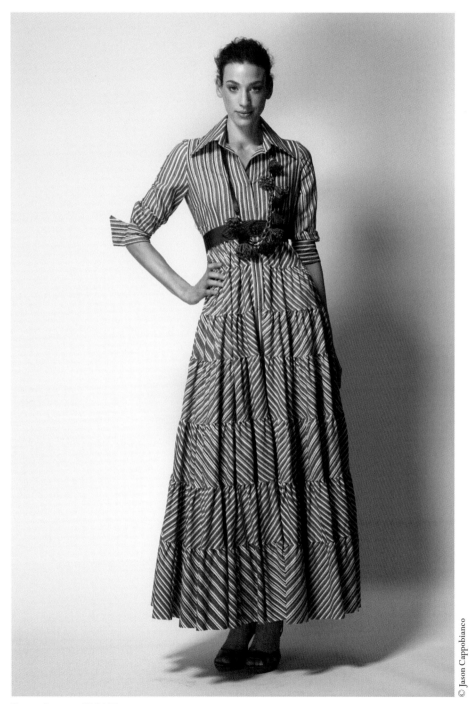

Easton Pearson SS 2007 www.eastonpearson.com

Edwina Hörl AW 2006-2007 www.edwinahoerl.com

Photo © Seiji Shibuya; art direction: so+ba; styling: Kumiko Iijima/Cube; hair: Miki Katsuhara; make-up: Lyar/Juice;

Edwina Hörl AW 2006-2007 www.edwinahoerl.com

Shirts, T-shirts and tops

Sleeveless top

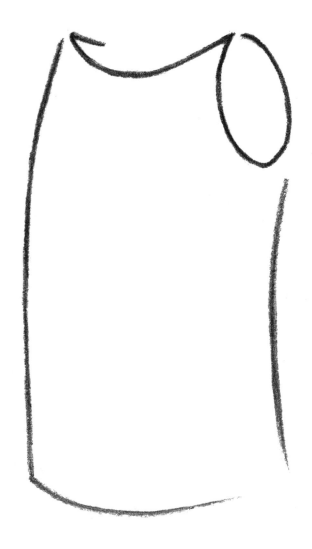

Easton Pearson SS 2007 www.eastonpearson.com

Yiyí Gutz SS 2008 www.yiyigutz.es, www.myspace.com/yiyigutz

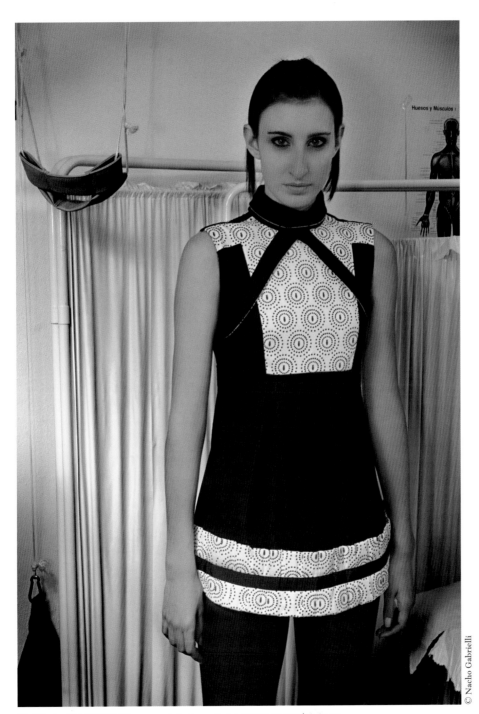

Yiyí Gutz AW 2007-2008 www.yiyigutz.es, www.myspace.com/yiyigutz

T-shirt

Carolina Restrepo/PUROCORAZÓN SS 2008 www.mipurocorazon.com

Photo © Camilo Echeverri; production: Bibiana Mesa; make-up: Juliana González; model: Liliana Torres

Avsh Alom Gur SS 2006 www.avshalomgur.com

© Vanessa Ellis

c.neeon AW 2007·2008 cneeon.de

© Alex Kohout

Ashish AW 2007-2008 www.ashish.co.uk

Ashish

Which colors stand out the most in your collections?
I love color. For the winter collection the colors were jewel like – very rich, vibrant and glowing – and lots of metallic as well. For summer the palette was more subdued, a lot of pale washed out color, muddy tones and neutrals.

What are your sources of inspiration?
My inspiration comes from lots of different sources: movies, books, my friends, flea markets, cities, nature, comics and found objects. And of course, I love palettes in every color, shape and size.

Which is your favorite color?
Every day it's a different one.

Boat-neck top

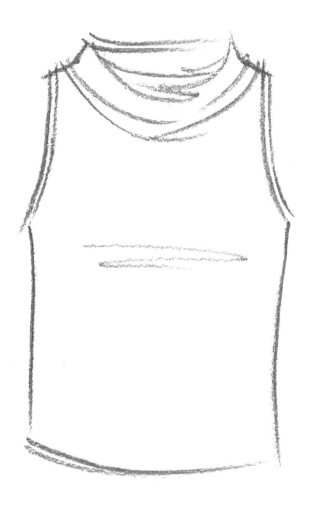

Easton Pearson SS 2007 www.eastonpearson.com

Easton Pearson SS 2007 www.eastonpearson.com

© Jason Cappobianco

Easton Pearson

Which colors stand out the most in your collections?
For the last few seasons we have used acid yellow, blues, greens and reds as highlight colors in our collections.

What are your sources of inspiration?
Because we live in a hot climate, the light is very clear and the landscape has vivid colors, so it is natural that this inspires our work. We are currently working with two local artists whose use of color has informed the latest collections. We spend time in India and Vietnam and are influenced by both the color on the street and in the way artists and artisans use it in their work. We love to highlight intense colors against a base of the neutral ones of the earth.

Which is your favorite color?
We could not name a favorite color, as they do not exist in a void, but change according to the context in which they are perceived.

Long-sleeved T-shirt

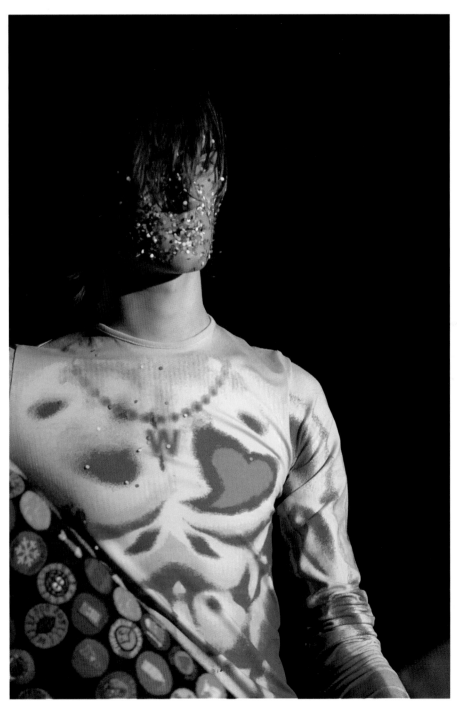

Walter Van Beirendonck AW 2006-2007 www.waltervanbeirendonck.com

Easton Pearson SS 2007 www.eastonpearson.com

Avsh Alom Gur SS 2006 www.avshalomgur.com

© Vanessa Ellis

Bernhard Willhelm Women's collection, SS 2008 www.totemfashion.com

Bernhard Willhelm

Which colors stand out the most in your collections?
It's more the combination of color contrasts: green-white, black-white-pink-red, blue-black, etc... Creating a tension between colors.

What are your sources of inspiration?
All the things we love:
– Birds flying towards us and then flying away again.
– The moments between moments, when you're happy.
– Cafes with two guests and a dog.
– Streets made of golden sunlight.
– Meat and dumplings at home.
– The high of sex.
– A lot of money when we earn it, not later when we spend it.
– Art at the moment it's created.
– Something very expensive that we can afford.
– A certain smile.
– Elephant showers.
– Death, as long as we're not dying.

Which is your favorite color?
Kardinal rot.

Classic shirt

MIHARAYASUHIRO SS 2008 www.sosu.co.jp

MIHARAYASUHIRO SS 2008 www.sosu.co.jp

Claudia Rosa Lukas AW 2005-2006 www.lukas-by.com

Photo © Michael Dürr; model: Hanna Putz

Hampus Bernhoff AW 2008-2009 www.hampusbernhoff.com

Hampus Bernhoff AW 2008-2009 www.hampusbernhoff.com

Fabrics Interseason SS 2007 www.fabrics.at

© Maria Ziegelböck

Alexis Mabille AW 2007-2008 www.alexismabille.com

Victorian blouse

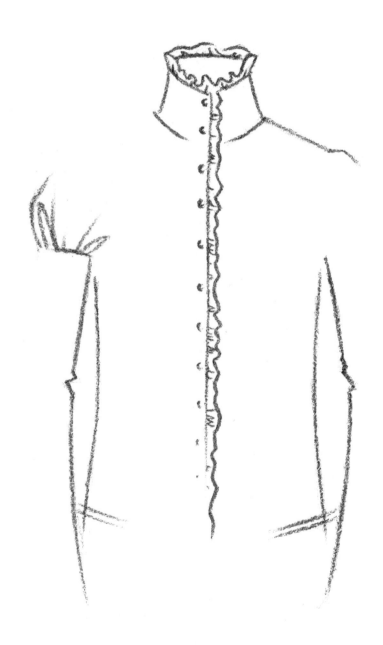

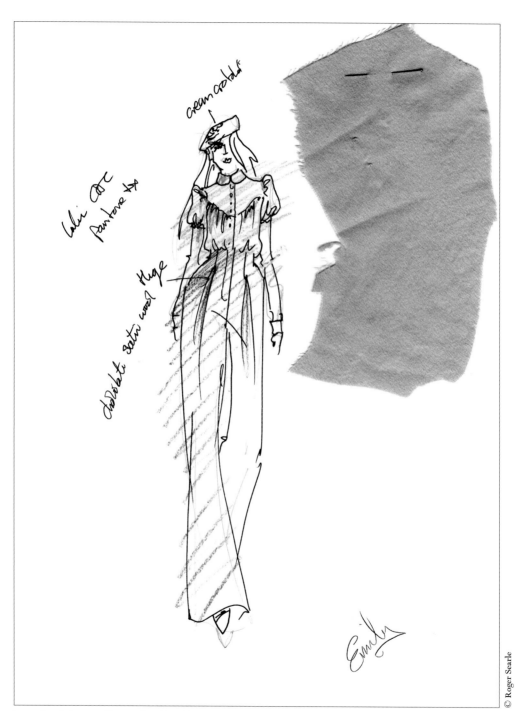

cream coctolet

celi CdC
Pantone tx

chocolate satin wool Mage

Roger Searle for Camilla Staerk *The Influence of Ghosts*, AW 2007-2008 www.camillastaerk.co.uk

Hildur Yeoman *The Bow Collection* www.hilduryeoman.com

IVANAhelsinki AW 2008-2009 www.ivanahelsinki.com

© Ivo Corda

Ana Šekularac AW 2008-2009 www.anasekularac.com

Ana Šekularac

Which colors stand out the most in your collections?
The signature colors are black and red, which I use in my collection
every season. On this canvas, I then add two new colors, both
complimentary and contrasting, thus reflecting the mood of each
particular season.

What are your sources of inspiration?
I draw inspiration from the world around myself, in particular
modern architecture, the arts, literature, illustrations and every genre
of art and artistic performances.
Each season, I combine in my work a historical period with a specific
genre. Art Deco, Modern Architecture or Renaissance Matador are
just a few examples in recent collections. My vision enables me to see
the link between subjects that may have no apparent connection and
to bring out the similarities between the chosen time period and the
specific genre whilst adding a uniquely modern yet timeless and
individual touch.

Which is your favorite color?
I have two favorite ones: black and red. The color black conveys
elegance, sophistication and a touch of mystery. Red catches people's
attention and evokes the strongest reactions of all colors. Red carries a
largely positive connotation, being associated with courage, energy,
strength and determination, loyalty and honor, as well as emotions
such as happiness, passion and love.

Sweaters

Crew-neck sweater

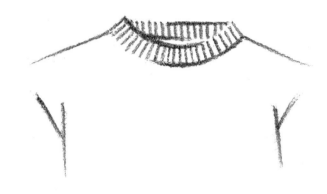

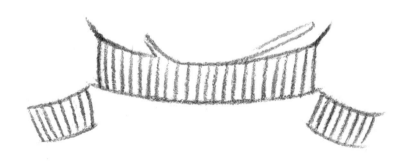

Walter Van Beirendonck SS 2008 www.waltervanbeirendonck.com

Fabrics Interseason SS 2007 www.fabrics.at

© Maria Ziegelböck

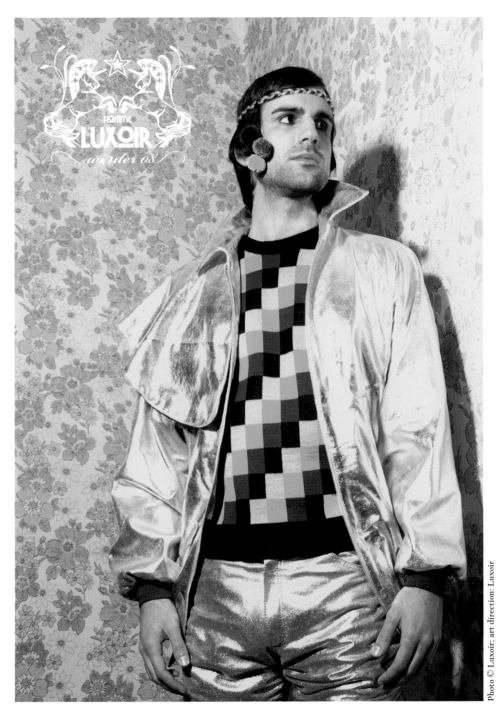

Luxoir *Junk*, AW 2007-2008 www.luxoir.com

Hartmann Nordenholz SS 2006 www.hartmannnordenholz.com

Hartmann Nordenholz

Which colors stand out the most in your collections?
Color is used as a monochrome block: neon pink, royal blue, golden beige and black are the strong and clear colors of this collection AW 2007/2008.

What are your sources of inspiration?
A connection between theory and high craftsmanship is the base of Hartmann Nordenholz. Fashion is a mean for personal expression and development. Each of our collections is a moment's glimpse of our "diary of reflections". Distance, silence and dignity are important keywords. Our approach is a critical one, in the sense of questioning different forms of fashion's as they appear in society. As result of our conceptual work, there has to be a perfect product.

Which is your favorite color?
Gray. As there is a lack of color, it is neutral. That's a good base to add color.

Long v-neck sweater

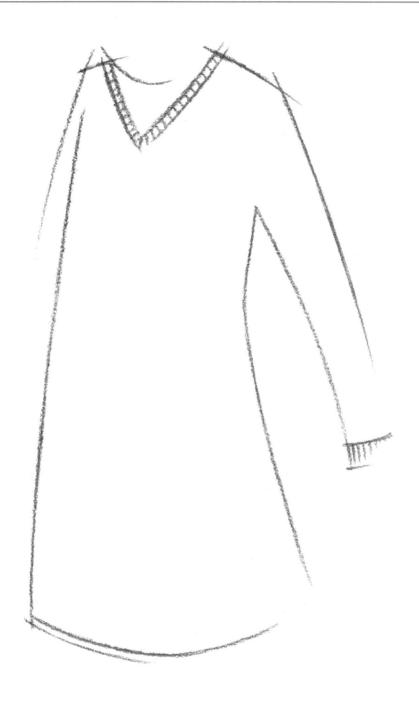

Hartmann Nordenholz SS 2006 www.hartmannnordenholz.com

Yiorgos Eleftheriades AW 2007-2008 www.yiorgoseleftheriades.gr

Yiorgos Eleftheriades

Which colors stand out the most in your collections?
Electric blue – which is a color that I love and use a lot in my work – ,
mocha, beige, antelope, emerald green and ultra violet.

What are your sources of inspiration?
I have a way of seeing the world around me in a voyeuristic way.
People from all over the world, in urban surroundings, large cities; a
universe of different cultures, opposites that coexist and ultimately
complement each other, all aesthetically offer a mosaic of textures and
colors. I find my personal day-to-day environment equally inspiring
with its sounds and music. The future and the path of evolution are
also important. They are the reason I tend to look ahead.

Which is your favorite color?
Blue is the color that relaxes me and makes me feel. I consider it a
neutral color, which seems to combine very easily with the rest of my
palette.

Turtle-neck sweater

Allegra Hicks AW 2008-2009 www.allegrahicks.com

Photo © Al De Perez; model: Margaret Clunie

Belinda Robertson AW 2008-2009 www.belindarobertson.com

© Chris Blott

IVANAhelsinki AW 2008-2009 www.ivanahelsinki.com

Cardigan

Tata-Naka AW 2007-2008 www.tatanaka.com

Easton Pearson SS 2007 www.eastonpearson.com

Sunshine & Shadow AW 2006-2007 www.sunshineandshadow.com

Zip-up jacket with collar

MIHARAYASUHIRO SS 2008 www.sosu.co.jp

Carolina Restrepo/PUROCORAZÓN SS 2008 www.mipurocorazon.com

PUROCORAZÓN

Which colors stand out the most in your collections?
I use a great deal of fuchsia in all its hues and variations, from rose through to cherry. The blending of dark shades such as brown and black with bright colors is one of the PUROCORAZÓN formulas.

What are your sources of inspiration?
My greatest inspiration is Peru, its customs, landscape and traditional dress. My visits to this country fill me with ideas on shape and color.

What is your favorite color?
I don't have a special favorite nor could I define myself by one — it would be a crime. I think that colors are marvelous — they are all an integral part of my life and work.

Hooded sweatshirt

Beige AW 2007-2008 www.beige.ch

© Daniel Sutter

EMDAL colorknit *Mau*, AW 2007-2008 www.emdalcolorknit.dk

Luxoir *Mirage*, SS 2008   www.luxoir.com

Walter Van Beirendonck AW 2006-2007 www.waltervanbeirendonck.com

EMDAL colorknit *Mau*, AW 2007-2008 www.emdalcolorknit.dk

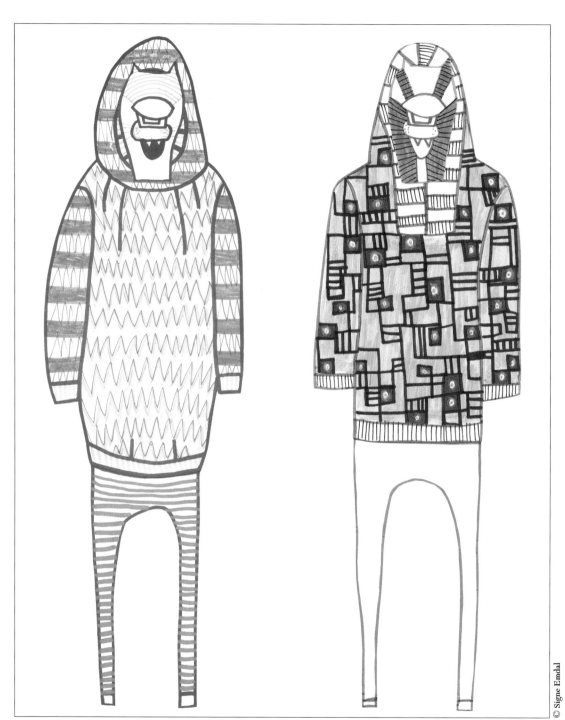

EMDAL colorknit *Mau*, AW 2007-2008 www.emdalcolorknit.dk

EMDAL colorknit

Which colors stand out the most in your collections?
EMDAL colorknit is all about yarns, stories and color. My world of colors
comes from a secret place inside of me, but I always try to be true to the
specific concept I'm currently working at. The story sets the limits, also
the color limits. Outstanding colors have always been one of the greatest
issues in my life. Everywhere around me I see amazing colors floating. I
need to work along with these colors; otherwise I don't feel happy inside.
It's hard to explain, but it's just "meant to be" that I'm working with
colors. :-)

What are your sources of inspiration?
My brand is built on storytelling, for example the one about the old
Egyptian cat-goddess Bastet. I am drowned in cultural and geographical
history, and I always express the stories through my knitted concepts.

Which is your favorite color?
For me, no color can stand and live on its own. I have about four favorite
colors – one or all of them most often occur with other changing colors,
depending on the current concept. These four colors are: coral-red,
ultramarine blue, bright yellow and black-black. They all make me happy.
They bring out memories from my childhood and float in my mind all the
time. When my pencil box doesn't have a fresh pencil in these four colors,
it's hard for me to do drawings. Of course, everybody's favorite colors
change from time to time. Next year I will maybe have one or maybe six
favorite colors. :-)

Sweatshirt

Mehdi Hercberg/SHOBOSHOBO *Black Swamp* www.shoboshobo.com

Tina Vanda Schou, Sofie Edvard Nielsen/DEVANDERVAR AW 2008-2009 www.devandervar.dk

DEVANDERVAR

Which colors stand out the most in your collections?
With colors like gray, ochre and dark green we have looked for a more subdued expression.

What are your sources of inspiration?
Everyday life, ordinary people. Everything happens in the process of experiment.

Which is your favorite color?
We love every color. It is when you start combining them that the magic happens.

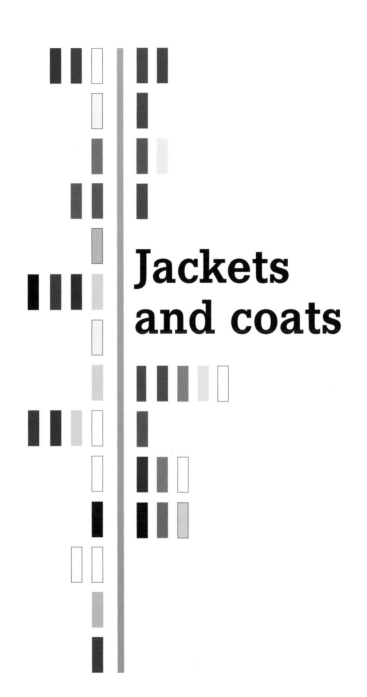

Jackets
and coats

Tailored jacket

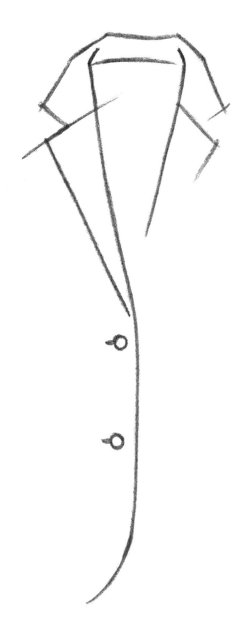

Photo © Matthew Shave; styling; Caroline Charles Team; hair; Christiano Bascui using Bobbi Brown; make-up: Angela Davis-Deacon; model: Inga Rogachenko/Models; jewelry: Coleman Douglas Pearls

Caroline Charles SS 2008 www.carolinecharles.co.uk

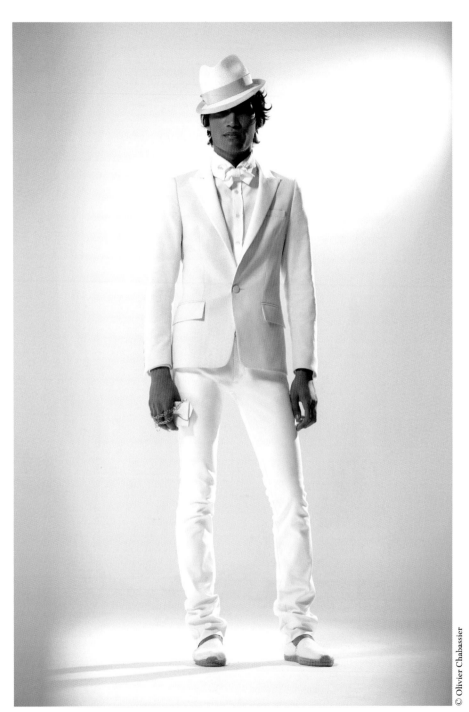

Alexis Mabille SS 2008 www.alexismabille.com

Steve J & Yoni P SS 2008 www.stevejandyonip.com

Duckie Brown AW 2007-2008 www.duckiebrown.com

© Steven Cox

Wooyoungmi SS 2007 www.wooyoungmi.com

Alexis Mabille AW 2007-2008 www.alexismabille.com

Alexis Mabille

Which colors stand out the most in your collections?
Nothing in particular, it's the sensation you have at the time.

What are your sources of inspiration?
People, life and a desire to entertain myself.

Which is your favorite color?
Every color...

Mao collar jacket

Caroline Charles SS 2008 www.carolinecharles.co.uk

Wooyoungmi AW 2006-2007 www.wooyoungmi.com

Wooyoungmi

Which colors stand out the most in your collections?
My outstanding colors are red, yellow, blue and orange.

What are your sources of inspiration?
I usually get inspiration from other aesthetic subjects, for example architecture, the arts and photography.

Which is your favorite color?
My favorite color is black because it makes our styles clean and chic.

1940's style jacket

Mac Millan SS 2008 www.mac-millan.com

Ana Šekularac AW 2008-2009 www.anasekularac.com

Ana Šekularac AW 2008-2009 www.anasekularac.com

Jose Castro SS 2008 www.castroestudio.com

Ana Šekularac SS 2008 www.anasekularac.com

Bolero jacket

Olivia Rubin SS 2008 www.oliviarubinlondon.com

Hildur Yeoman *The Bow Collection* www.hilduryeoman.com

Hildur Yeoman *The Bow Collection* www.hilduryeoman.com

229

Pea jacket

Evie Belle SS 2008 www.eviebelle.com

Photo © Paul Gore; styling: Sairah Hicks; hair and make-up: Beth Roberts Miller; model: Brook/FM

A&V AW 2007-2008 www.lithill.lt/a&v

© Paulius Gasiunas

Duckie Brown AW 2007-2008 www.duckiebrown.com

© Platon

Duckie Brown AW 2007-2008 www.duckiebrown.com

© Platon

Duckie Brown

Which colors stand out the most in your collections?
Green, yellow, red and blue.

What are your sources of inspiration?
The lives we lead.

Which is your favorite color?
Steven's favorite color is turquoise and red is my favorite color
[Daniel].

Trench coat

Photo © Modestas Ezerskis; model: Aiste Jasaityte

Ashish AW 2007-2008 www.ashish.co.uk

Ashish AW 2007-2008 www.ashish.co.uk